BABY MEDICAL SCHOOL

BACTERIA and ANTIBIOTICS

By Margot and Antonis Alesund

FROM THE CREATOR OF THE BABY BIOCHEMIST

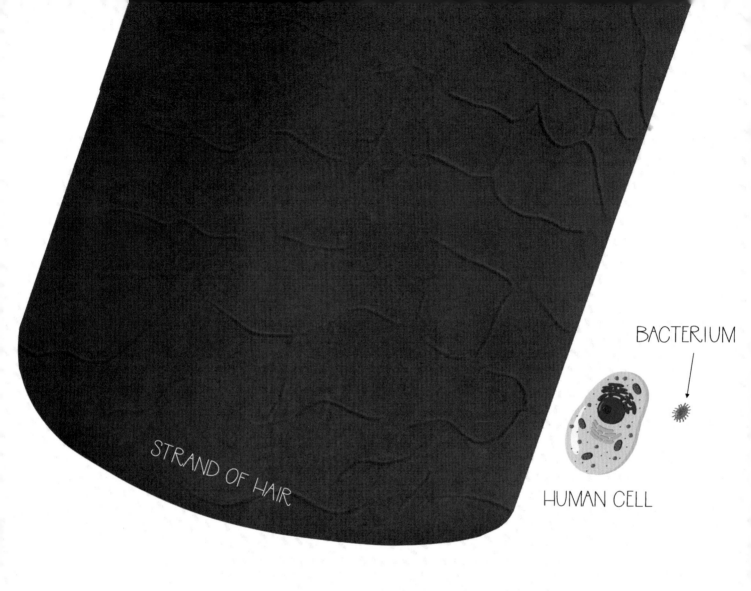

STRAND OF HAIR

BACTERIUM

HUMAN CELL

Bacteria are very small living things.

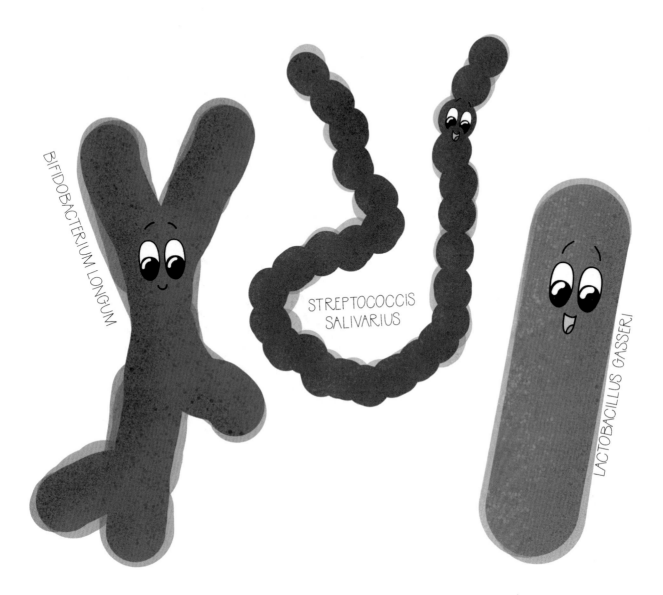

BIFIDOBACTERIUM LONGUM

STREPTOCOCCIS
SALIVARIUS

LACTOBACILLUS GASSERI

Your body has lots of bacteria in it and on it. This is called your microbiome.

Some of those bacteria can
be good or bad for us.

And sometimes those bad bacteria can take over, making you sick.

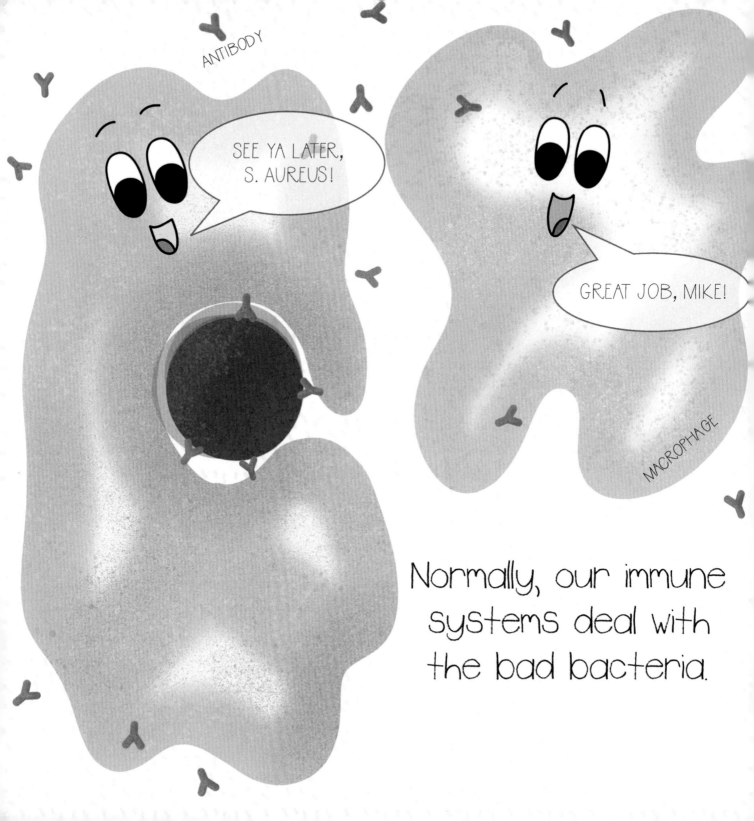

But sometimes, things can get out of control and our bodies need help.

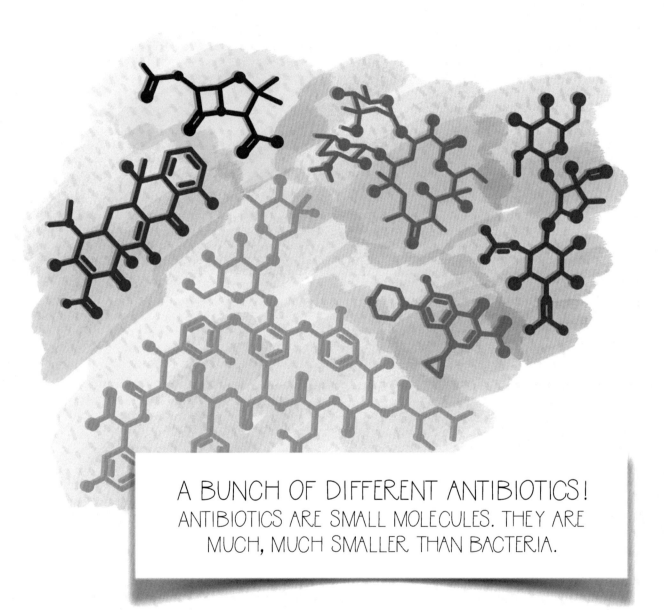

A BUNCH OF DIFFERENT ANTIBIOTICS!
ANTIBIOTICS ARE SMALL MOLECULES. THEY ARE
MUCH, MUCH SMALLER THAN BACTERIA.

Luckily we have a family of medicine, called antibiotics, that can get rid of bacteria.

There are several types of antibiotics that target different parts and different types of bacteria.

Many of the antibiotics we use were originally found in bacteria and fungi.

They need antibiotics to protect themselves, too!

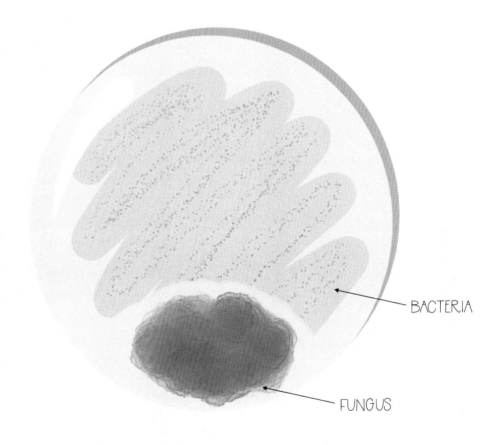

BACTERIA

FUNGUS

Our first antibiotic was discovered by accident when a mold (a type of fungus) mysteriously stopped bacteria growth in a petri dish.

The mold was making penicillin! This famous antibiotic stops an "enzyme" that helps build the bacteria's cell wall. We now use penicillin to help people!

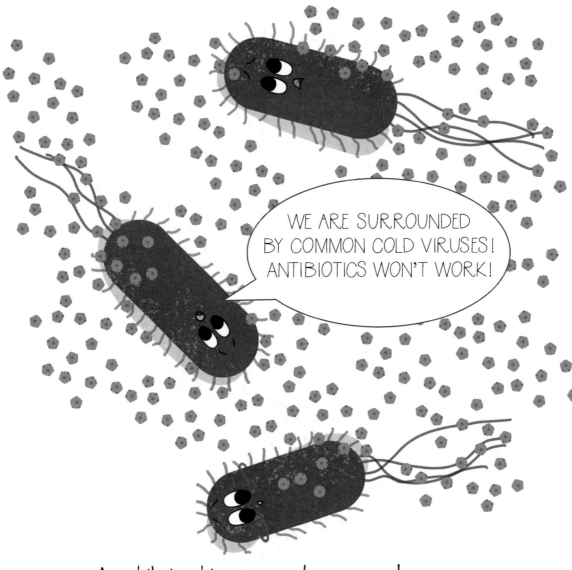

Antibiotics only work on
bacteria. They will not get rid
of viruses or fungi.

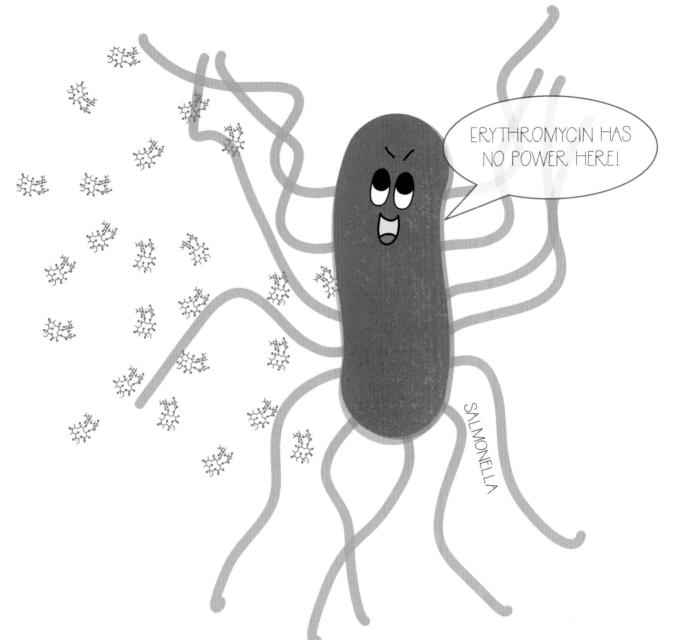

And not all antibiotics work
on all bacteria.

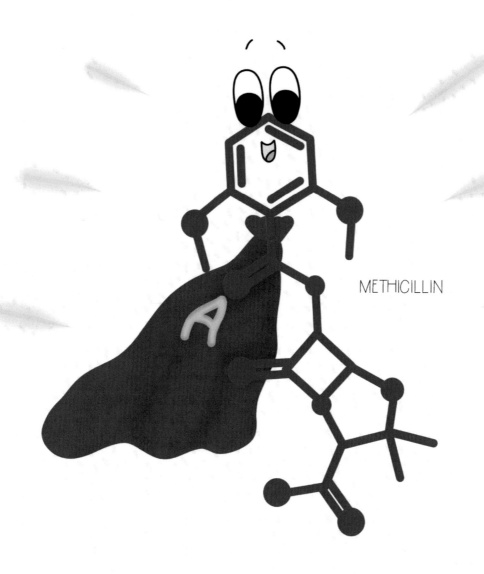

METHICILLIN

Antibiotics have saved many people's lives...

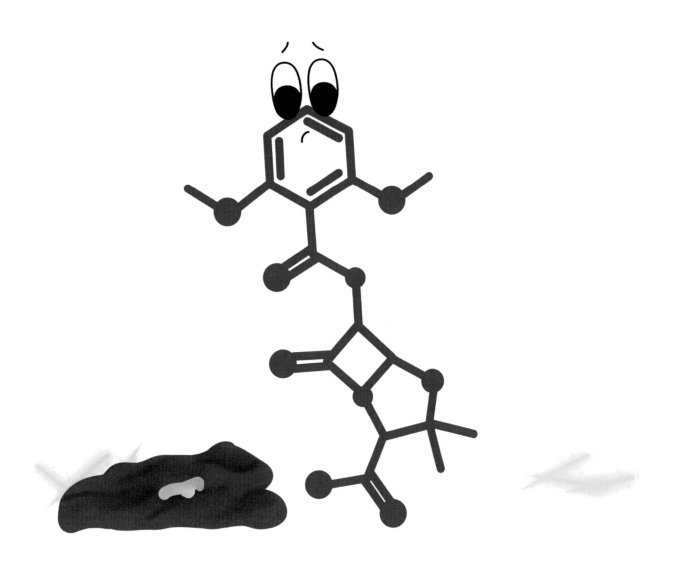

...but lately we've been having
some trouble with them.

Some bacteria have found ways to "outsmart" antibiotics, like making an enzyme that cuts penicillin! This is called antibiotic resistance.

The cut penicillin will not stick to the cell wall enzyme, so the bacteria can still build the wall and keep on living!

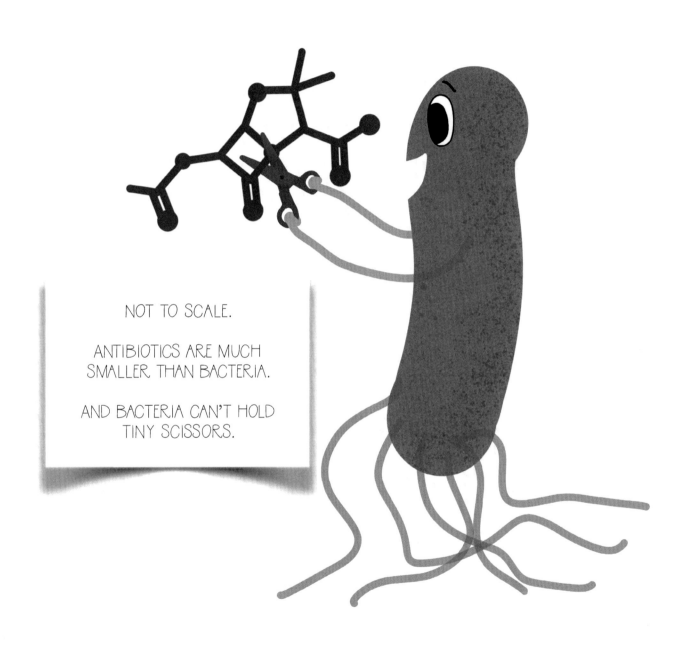

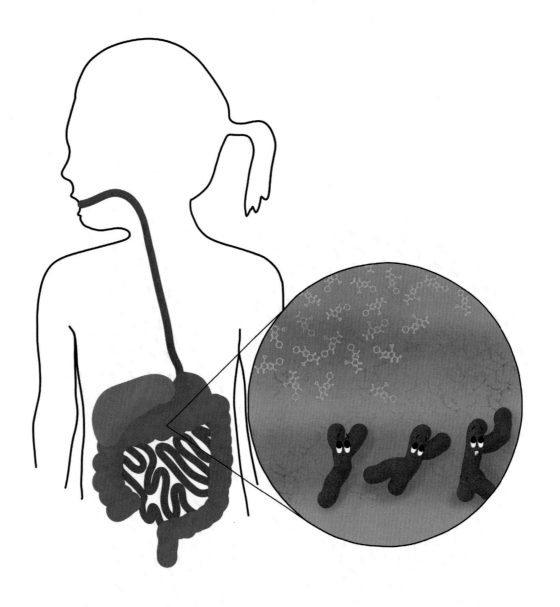

Another problem is that antibiotics also remove our good bacteria!

And the good bacteria in our bodies are VERY important to staying healthy.

Doctors and scientists are learning how to properly help return good bacteria to your body. These are called probiotics.

(But keep in mind, there is lots
of bad information about
probiotics out there.)

We are learning more about the
bacteria in our bodies every day!

Maybe you can help by becoming a
doctor or scientist!

Congratulations on completing

Bacteria and Antibiotics: 101

Check out other books from:

Baby Medical School

And

THE BABY BIOCHEMIST

Made in the USA
San Bernardino, CA
05 March 2018